HILLS AND MOUNTAINS

BRENDA WILLIAMS

HODDER
Wayland

an imprint of Hodder Children's Books

GEOGRAPHY STARTS HERE!

Hills and Mountains

OTHER TITLES IN THE SERIES
Maps and Symbols · Rivers and Streams
Weather Around You · Where People Live
Your Environment

Produced for Wayland Publishers Limited by
Lionheart Books
10, Chelmsford Square
London NW10 3AR
England

Designer: Ben White

Editor: Lionel Bender

Picture Research: Madeleine Samuel

Electronic make-up: Mike Pilley, Radius.

Illustrated by Rudi Visi and Peter Bull

First published in Great Britain in 1997
by Wayland (Publishers) Ltd
Reprinted in 2002 by Hodder Wayland,
an imprint of Hodder Children's Books
© Hodder Wayland 1997

British Library Cataloguing in Publication Data

Williams, Brenda

Hills and mountains. – (Geography starts here!)

1. Mountains – Juvenile literature

I. Title II. Bender, Lionel

551.4'3

ISBN 0 7502 4158 6

Printed and bound in Hong Kong

Picture Acknowledgements
Pages 1: GeoScience Features Picture Library. 5: GeoScience Features Picture Library. 7: Zefa
Photo Library. 8: Zefa Photo Library/H. Weyer. 9: Zefa Photo Library. 10-11: Zefa Photo Library.
12: Wayland Picture Library. 13: Zefa Photo Library. 14: GeoScience Features Picture Library.
15: DAS Photos/David Simson. 16: Zefa Photo Library/Stockmarket. 18-19: Zefa Photo
Library/Stockmarket/ S. G. Drinker. 20: Eye Ubiquitous/J. B. Pickering. 21: DAS Photos/David
Simson. 22: Eye Ubiquitous/Dean Bennett. 23: Eye Ubiquitous/Paul Thompson. 24-25: Zefa
Photo Library. 26: James Davis Travel Photography. 27: Zefa Photo Library. 28: Tony Stone
Worldwide/Oli Tennet. 29: Lionheart Books. 31: Wayland Picture Library.

The photo on the previous page shows a view over the Alps in Switzerland.

CONTENTS

HIGH AND MIGHTY

A mountain is a mass of rock that rises high above the land around it. At its top it may be so cold that no plants grow there. A hill is lower than a mountain. Grass and trees may grow on hilltops.

Mountains form slowly, over millions of years, and are then worn away by wind, rain and snow. Some mountains are made when hot, liquid rock pours out of the Earth. These mountains are called volcanoes.

The world's tallest mountains form huge areas of high ground called ranges or chains.

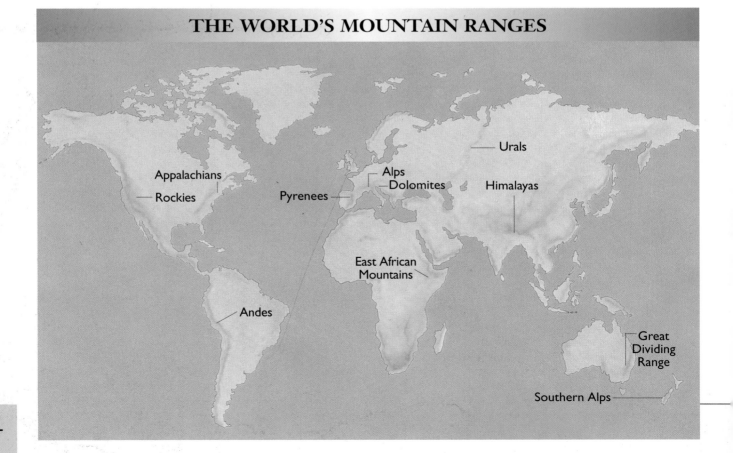

THE WORLD'S MOUNTAIN RANGES

Appalachians

Rockies

Pyrenees

Alps
Dolomites

Urals

Himalayas

East African Mountains

Andes

Great Dividing Range

Southern Alps

A hotel stands at the bottom of a mountain summit in the Dolomites, Italy.

HOW MOUNTAINS FORM

The Earth has a skin called the crust. This is made of huge plates of rock that fit together like the pieces of a giant jigsaw.

The continents, or masses of land, rest on some of the plates. Oceans cover all the other plates.

The plates in the Earth's crust move about. When these plates bump together, the rock between the plates is forced upwards and folds in on itself. This creates fold mountains.

MAKING FOLD MOUNTAINS

You can see how fold mountains form by pushing together the ends of a large sheet of paper. Your hands act like the forces of two plates of the crust bumping into each other.

Tourists enjoy the view over a range of mountains in Yosemite National Park, California, USA.

Highest and Newest

The world's tallest mountain range is the Himalayas in Asia. The mountains are steep-sided and jagged, and their summits are permanently covered in snow.

This is the summit of Mount Everest, the highest mountain in the world.

The two plates of crust that collided and formed the Himalayas are still moving together. Here, the Earth is making new mountains. In the same way, new mountains are forming in the Alps in Europe and in the Andes in South America.

A railway runs alongside the Alps mountains in Switzerland.

Cracks and Faults

From inside the Earth, great pressures push against the crust. Sometimes they tear mountains apart or cause cracks in the rock. Large cracks are called faults.

Between the faults, huge blocks of rock may be forced up. This is how mountains in the Black Forest region of Europe and in the Sierra Nevada of North America were formed.

Sharp, jagged peaks caused by faults in the Dolomites mountains in Italy.

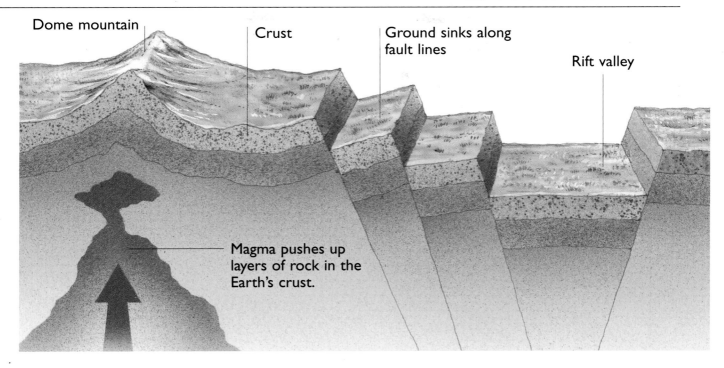

Dome mountain   Crust   Ground sinks along fault lines   Rift valley

Magma pushes up layers of rock in the Earth's crust.

▲ Underneath the Earth's crust lies hot, liquid rock called magma. When magma is forced upwards, faults and rift valleys are created.

WEARING AWAY

Mountains crumble even while they are being made. They are warmed by sunshine and cool at night. This weakens and cracks the rock. The cracks fill with water that freezes to ice. Ice widens the cracks, and the rocks split and crumble.

Rivers erode, or wear away, rock. They form giant valleys in the land. As glaciers slide down mountainsides, they grind away rock and carve out hollows.

These mounds of rock in Australia have been worn smooth by wind and rain.

This mountainside in Wales has been eroded by wind, rain and ice.

Hills and Stumps

In time, mountains turn into hills. The hardest rocks take longest to erode. Lumps of such hard rock as granite may be left sticking up as stumps after the rest of a mountain has crumbled and worn away.

This strange, moon-like landscape on hills in Wyoming, USA, was caused by erosion of rock.

Some hills are formed from mounds of soil or loose rocks piled up by melting glaciers. Others are formed by rivers dropping mud and other material.

On a hillside in France, soft rock has been worn away by rain and wind, leaving ridges of hard rock.

VOLCANOES

Volcanoes are special types of mountains. Red-hot, molten rock called lava spouts from the crater, or hole, in their tops.

The world has around 850 volcanoes that may erupt at any time. Many of them are under the sea. Most are on 'hot-spots' of the Earth's crust, where plates collide and new fold mountains are growing.

A volcano erupts on the island of Hawaii. Gases and ash shoot up from the crater along with hot, molten rock.

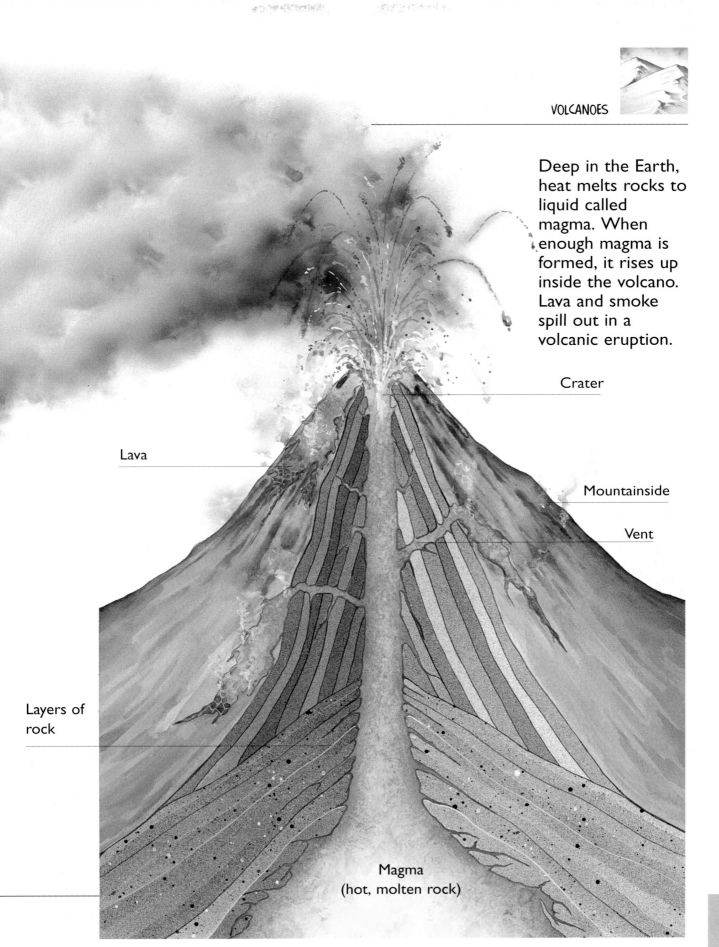

Deep in the Earth, heat melts rocks to liquid called magma. When enough magma is formed, it rises up inside the volcano. Lava and smoke spill out in a volcanic eruption.

Crater

Lava

Mountainside

Vent

Layers of rock

Magma
(hot, molten rock)

Alive or Dead?

Lava cools and hardens as it flows away from a volcano. As layers of lava build up, the cone-shaped mountain grows bigger and bigger.

Some volcanoes are 'active' – they rumble and puff gas almost all the time. Others are 'dormant' – they stay quiet for many years between eruptions. 'Extinct' volcanoes are not expected to erupt again.

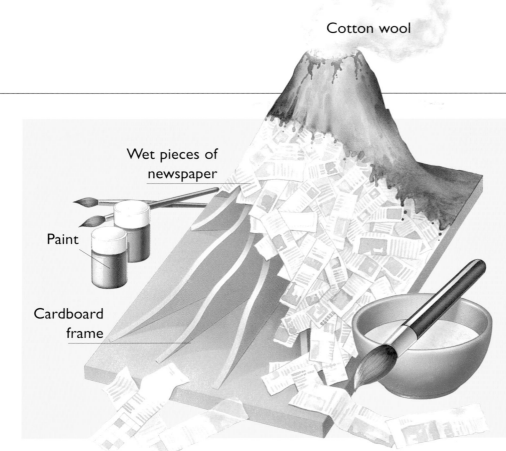

Cotton wool

Wet pieces of newspaper

Paint

Cardboard frame

BUILD A MODEL VOLCANO

Make the frame of the volcano using pieces of cardboard stuck on a baseboard. Lay small squares or strips of wet newspaper over the frame to make the sides of the volcano. When the paper is dry and hard, paint your volcano using water-colour paints.

An extinct volcano on Hawaii. Water has filled the crater, and lush plants grow on the mountainsides.

ON TOP OF THE WORLD

A road zigzags down a mountainside in Italy. A straight road would be too steep for vehicles to drive up.

Few people live on high mountains. The cold winds and poor soil make it difficult to grow crops there. Steep slopes make building houses and travel difficult. Mountain people are mostly poor and lead a hard life.

In Ecuador, South America, people load a truck with goods to take to their village in the Andes mountains.

Where the weather is not too harsh, many people live on hills. Most of them are farmers. They live in houses and rural settlements often very long distances away from their nearest neighbours.

Terraces in the Philippine islands. Here, the famers grow rice.

Mountain Farming

Mountain people make extra farmland by cutting wide steps, called terraces, into the slopes. Terraces also stop rain washing away soil. The farmers grow rice, potatoes, barley, maize and wheat, and keep goats and sheep.

On hillsides in warm countries such as India and Sri Lanka, farmers grow tea, coffee and cotton plants. Where the weather is cooler, farmers keep herds of sheep, goats and cattle on hillsides.

Sheep graze beside a lake on hills in Wales.

High Life

Mountain plants hug the ground, out of the biting cold wind. Long roots stop the plants being blown away. The wind bends trees into strange shapes.

No trees grow above a certain height on a mountain. This 'tree-line' is highest on mountains in warm countries.

On mountain slopes where it is warm and damp, plants such as ivy, mosses and ferns cover the branches and trunks of trees.

On high mountains in warm regions of the world, such as Mount Kilimanjaro in East Africa, different types of plants grow at each level. Snow covers the summit all year round.

Snow-line

Alpine meadow

Tree-line

Coniferous and deciduous forests

Tropical rain forest

Grassland

Mountain Animals

On mountains, there are few places for animals to find shelter and food. On the highest peaks only insects and spiders live on the ground, but birds such as eagles and condors soar high above.

The climate on hills is usually warmer. Hills are homes all sorts of animals, from sheep and goats to snakes and spiders.

People with llamas in the Andes mountains. Llamas are kept for their thick wool, their creamy milk and to carry heavy loads.

Bighorn cattle graze on hills in the Rocky Mountains in the USA.

A climber looks for a
foothold as he clambers
up a rockface.

MOUNTAINS FOR FUN

Mountains are among the world's last wild places. But more people are visiting them than ever before, to ski, climb, walk or hang glide.

Our mountains need to be looked after. We must protect them from the damage that lots of visitors can cause. Walkers, skiers and mountainbikers can all damage mountains and hillsides. But with care, these beautiful areas will last millions of years more.

A ski resort in the Pyrenees Mountains in Europe. Skiing is the most popular mountain sport.

MOUNTAIN FACTS AND FIGURES

The world's highest mountains

Asia
Everest (Tibet, China-Nepal)
8,848 metres

South America
Aconcagua (Argentina)
6,959 metres

North America
McKinley (Alaska, USA)
6,194 metres

Africa
Kilimanjaro (Tanzania)
5,895 metres

Europe
Elbrus (Russia) 5,642 metres

Australia
Kosciusko 2,228 metres

Famous mountains

Ararat (Turkey) 5,185 metres.
Said to be the resting place of
Noah's Ark.

Matterhorn
(Swiss-Italian Alps)
4,478 metres.
First scaled in 1865 by Edward
Whymper of Britain.

**K2, also called Godwin
Austen or Dapsang**
(Karakoram range, Asia).
World's second highest
mountain (8,611 metres)
First climbed in 1954.

Olympus (Greece)
2,917 metres.
Traditional home of the gods
of ancient Greece.

Fujiyama (Japan)
3,776 metres.
Sacred mountain of Japan.

Famous volcanoes

Mount St. Helens
(Washington, USA).
Volcano which killed 57 people
when it erupted in 1980.

Vesuvius (Italy).
Only active volcano on
mainland Europe. In 79 BC it
erupted and destroyed the
Roman towns of Herculaneum
and Pompeii.

Krakatau (Indonesia).
Volcano erupted in 1883
producing an enormous
explosion heard over 4,000 km
away, and caused an ocean wave
that killed about 36,000 people.

Mont Pelée (Martinique).
Volcano erupted in 1902
producing a gas cloud which
killed about 38,000 people.

Cotopaxi (Ecuador).
Volcano erupted in 1877,
producing a mud-flood that
spread more than 200 km and
killed about 1,000 people.

Further Reading

Jump! Ecology – Mountains (Two
Can, 1991).

Highest, Longest, Deepest by
John Malam and Gary Hincks
(Heinemann, 1996).

Planet Earth by Lionel Bender
(Kingfisher Books, 1991).

Planet Earth (Oxford University
Press, 1993).

The Changing Earth by Dougal
Dixon (Wayland, 1992).

Volcano by John Dudman
(Wayland, 1992).

CD Roms
Violent Earth (Wayland, 1996)
Exploring Land Habitats
(Wayland, 1997)

GLOSSARY

Ash The grey powder left behind when something has been burned.

Climate The sort of weather that a place usually gets at different times of the year.

Continent A very large piece of land. The Earth has seven continents – South America, North America, Europe, Africa, Asia, Oceania and Antarctica.

Crust The outer surface, skin or shell of the Earth. It is about 35–45 kilometres thick.

Fault A weak spot in the crust, where the ground cracks as a result of being pulled and pushed by rock movements.

Fold An overlap or rippling of rock layers, as a result of pressure in the Earth's crust

Plate A part of the solid outer layer of the Earth, including the crust, which floats on a layer of hot, melted rocks.

Pressure Force caused by pushing on or against something.

Summit A word used to describe the peak, or top of a mountain.

Valley A V-shaped channel in the land shaped by movements of the rocks or by rivers and glaciers cutting a groove.

A skiing resort nestled between snow-covered mountains in Switzerland.

INDEX